Exploring
Infrastructure

# OUR WATER SUPPLY

Rita Santos

**Enslow Publishing**
101 W. 23rd Street
Suite 240
New York, NY 10011
USA

enslow.com

Published in 2020 by Enslow Publishing, LLC.
101 W. 23rd Street, Suite 240, New York, NY 10011

Copyright © 2020 by Enslow Publishing, LLC.

**Library of Congress Cataloging-in-Publication Data**

Names: Santos, Rita, author.
Title: Our water supply / Rita Santos.
Description: New York: Enslow Publishing, 2020. | Series: Exploring infrastructure | Includes bibliographical references and index. | Audience: Grades 3-6 |
Identifiers: LCCN 2018013650| ISBN 9781978503366 (library bound) | ISBN 9781978505117 (pbk.)
Subjects: LCSH: Water-supply—United States—Juvenile literature. |Infrastructure (Economics)—United States—Juvenile literature.
Classification: LCC TD223 .S26 2019 | DDC 628.10973—dc23
LC record available at https://lccn.loc.gov/2018013650

Printed in the United States of America

**To Our Readers:** We have done our best to make sure all website addresses in this book were active and appropriate when we went to press. However, the author and the publisher have no control over and assume no liability for the material available on those websites or on any websites they may link to. Any comments or suggestions can be sent by email to customerservice@enslow.com.

**Photo Credits:** Cover, p. 1 arhendrix/Shutterstock.com; cover, pp. 1, 3 (top) Panimoni/ Shutterstock.com; p. 4 mihalec/Shutterstock.com; p. 6 stockshoppe/Shutterstock.com; p. 9 Kean Collection/Archive Photos/Getty Images; p. 10 Hulton Archive/Archive Photos/ Getty Images; p. 13 Universal History Archive/Universal Images Group/Getty Images; p. 15 javarman/Shutterstock.com; p. 16 Designua/Shutterstock.com; p. 18 Aladdin Color Inc/ Corbis Historical/Getty Images; p. 21 David Dea/Shutterstock.com; p. 22 Bill Pugliano/ Getty Images; p. 25 Robert Nickelsberg/Archive Photos/Getty Images; p. 28 © AP Images; p. 29 The Washington Post/Getty Images; p. 31 Robyn Beck/AFP/Getty Images; p. 34 Michael Bocchieri/Getty Images; p. 35 Viliam.M/Shutterstock.com; p. 36 Justin Sullivan/ Getty Images; p. 39 Astrid Riecken/Getty Images; p. 41 Lonnie Duka/Photolibrary/Getty Images; p. 43 GuilhermeMesquita/Shutterstock.com.

# CONTENTS

Water is one of the basic needs for every living thing.

# INTRODUCTION

Without a regular supply of water, not much else in life gets done. In most American homes, it is easy to get clean water. Most people don't even think about it. Being able to get water affects everything from our health to our food supply. One of America's greatest successes is its water supply system. It is among the cleanest in the world. About a third of the world's population does not have access to clean drinking water. The World Health Organization estimates that three in ten people worldwide do not have safe drinking water in their home.

The typical American home uses about 70 gallons (265 liters) of water every day. People use water in their toilets, showers, washing machines, dishwashers, and faucets. Humans need to drink water to live. A person could live without food for about three weeks. Without water, a person could die in under a week. Water is one of the planet's most important resources. It is also a renewable resource. But this does not mean there is an endless supply. Our supply of safe drinking water could run out someday.

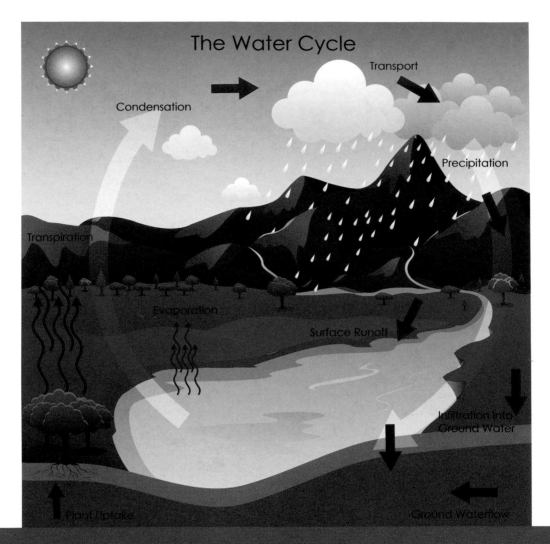

# The Water Cycle

Transport

Condensation

Precipitation

Transpiration

Evaporation

Surface Runoff

Infiltration Into Ground Water

Plant Uptake

Ground Waterflow

The water cycle shows us how water forms in clouds, falls to the ground as precipitation, and rises back up into the atmosphere.

Earth's water is in constant motion. Water evaporates as it is heated by the sun's rays. Then it rises into the atmosphere as vapor and forms clouds. When the clouds are full of water, the water falls to earth as rain, snow, or hail. This is called the water cycle. We depend on the water cycle to renew our supply of freshwater.

Today, most Americans get their water from publicly owned water systems. These systems move water from rivers and underground sources to treatment centers. There, the water is made safe to drink. Then it is moved to homes and businesses. This system of pipes and treatment centers is a part of our infrastructure.

"Infrastructure" is the term for the basic facilities and services that a community needs in order to function. This includes things like electricity, sewage, roads, hospitals, schools, and our water systems. All of these things are paid for using the taxes the government collects every year. A strong infrastructure is important for a community's success. Good infrastructure is needed to keep people safe and healthy.

It may seem like water is everywhere. But the more you learn about it, the more you will see how precious it is. Our water supply system is one of the most important pieces of America's infrastructure. Come learn about the history and future of this amazing system.

# Chapter One

# HISTORY OF THE AMERICAN WATER SUPPLY

People living in American cities in the 1700s did not have a bathroom in their homes. Instead, they used outdoor toilets. Waste ran into a gutter on the side of the street. In the early days, not too many people lived in the cities. But as more people arrived, there was a greater need for better sanitation. Sanitation is a way of making sure communities stay healthy. Getting rid of waste safely is an important part of sanitation. People knew they had to keep sewage away from drinking water. Drinking water usually came from rivers or wells that used water from the ground. But people did not know much else about how water could be contaminated.

People began using privy vaults and cesspools. These were large holes that were dug behind houses to store human waste. What

People get water from a well in New York City in the 1700s.

many people didn't realize was that the vaults and cesspools were not sanitary. They could easily contaminate water in the ground that was used for drinking. A lack of clean drinking water led to a lot of disease. In 1879, the city of Philadelphia checked seventy-one wells. Of those, thirty-three were filthy, ten were bad, twenty-two were suspicious, and six were good.

The cities grew larger. Local water sources were no longer enough to meet demands. Many cities built pipes to bring water

Workers build a new sewer system in Savannah, Georgia, in the 1890s.

from other places into people's homes. At the time, cities did not have separate sewage and water pipes. People would drop waste into the pipes that were only meant for drinking water. They did not realize they were contaminating their drinking water.

In the 1850s, people made the connection between contaminated water and disease. New sewer systems were built in Chicago and Brooklyn. These systems had different pipes for drinking water and sanitation. This also marked the start of placing bathrooms indoors. Some people were not happy about the cost of building the new system. They also thought that indoor plumbing would spread disease. However, access to clean water and proper sanitation is actually one of the best signs of health around the world.

Between the 1850s and 1900s, many new sewer and water systems were built. People soon saw that these systems were most effective when everyone had access to them. Public water systems and sanitation systems sprang up all over the country.

# Dangers of Untreated Water

Water can carry diseases and other elements that can make humans very sick. It can be contaminated with chemicals that can cause cancer, skin rashes, and brain issues. Sometimes water comes in contact with sewage or garbage. This can cause it to be contaminated with bacteria. Many illnesses found in water cause diseases that can lead to dehydration and death. Boiling water will kill most bacteria. But it will also raise the amount of dangerous heavy metals and salts. Every year, 3.4 million people around the world die of water-related illnesses. Most of these deaths could be prevented with access to clean water and sanitation.

America has one of the cleanest water supplies in the world.

## Cholera

Cholera is an illness that causes diarrhea. It can kill within hours if it is not treated. There have been seven cholera pandemics in history. Millions of people died. Cholera is easily spread through water. Access to clean water and sanitation has almost wiped out the disease in most countries. But sometimes water systems are damaged. This puts many people at risk. This happened in Yemen in 2016. Over a million Yemenis have become infected with cholera. Providing sanitation and clean water to people around the world is the best way to prevent cholera.

But there can still be contaminated water. In 2015, 113 people at a hospital in New York got sick. The hospital's water storage tanks had been contaminated. This type of event does not happen often. But it can remind us of just how dangerous a little bad water can be.

## What John Snow Knew

In 1854, an outbreak of cholera began in the Soho neighborhood of London. At the time, doctors thought that people got cholera by breathing in bad air. This was called the miasma theory. Doctor John Snow did not agree. He believed cholera was spread by drinking contaminated water.

Dr. Snow decided to find out where the infected people got their drinking water. He quickly discovered that most of the people who had died of the disease had drunk from one water pump. It was located on Broad Street. Dr. Snow explained his findings to the local government. He convinced them to remove the pump. This helped put an end to the epidemic.

As it turned out, the pump's well had been contaminated by an old cesspit. This was a hole for storing waste. The cesspit was only a few feet away from the well. Dr. Snow was able to confirm his theory when another cholera outbreak hit London. He traced the source of each house's drinking water. Each house got its water from one of two different water companies. One of the companies served mainly poor people. The company supplied the houses with water from a part of the river that was contaminated with sewage. The second company supplied water from a clean part of the river. Through this research, Dr. Snow was able to prove the connection between the contaminated water and the disease.

Today, Dr. Snow is considered the father of epidemiology. This is the study of how diseases are spread and what makes people sick. He showed how important it is to disinfect and filter water before drinking it. His discovery helped lead to safer water management.

A magazine cartoon shows children playing at a London water pump. The city water was the cause of cholera, a disease that killed hundreds of people.

# Chapter Two

# WHERE OUR WATER COMES FROM

Our oceans make up about 96 percent of the water on the earth. This means that most water is undrinkable for humans. People need a lot of water to live. They only need a small amount of salt. Seawater has more salt than the human body can break down. If you were to drink only seawater, you would soon die of dehydration.

Our drinking water comes from the earth's small supply of freshwater. This is water that doesn't contain a harmful amount of salt. Freshwater can come from places like rivers, lakes, and streams. In this chapter we'll explore how freshwater is collected and made safe to drink.

More than two-thirds of the planet is covered in water.
Unfortunately, most of that is salt water, so we cannot drink it.

## Groundwater and Freshwater

Community water is water that is used in apartments and businesses rather than in single-family homes. In the United States,
it comes from two main sources. Surface water is the water that
collects on the surface of the earth. This includes lakes and rivers.
About two-thirds of all community water comes from surface water.
When it rains, the supply of surface water is refreshed. Surface
water can also be lost. Sometimes it evaporates or seeps into the
earth and becomes groundwater.

Groundwater is all the water that is under the earth's surface. If
you were to dig deep enough, at some point you would hit the zone

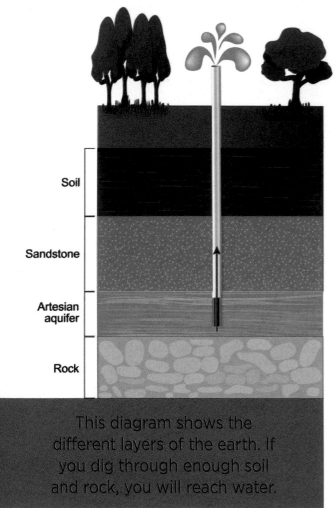

Soil

Sandstone

Artesian
aquifer

Rock

This diagram shows the different layers of the earth. If you dig through enough soil and rock, you will reach water.

of saturation. This is the point where the ground is full of, or saturated with, water. The water table is the line between the saturated and unsaturated earth. The water table can change based on the weather and how the land is used. A football field would have a higher water table than a parking lot. When it rains, a lot more water can seep into the football field than the concrete parking lot. When water cannot seep into the ground it's called runoff.

When water collects underground in rocks, it's known as an aquifer. The rocks in an aquifer allow some water to flow through them. The water in an aquifer is reached by digging wells that can pump the water out. Surface water that seeps into the earth ends up in aquifers. Almost 80 percent of American community water comes from groundwater. About 15 percent of Americans have private groundwater wells.

The supply of groundwater gets lower as it is used. Usually, the supply is refilled when it rains and more water seeps into the ground. This is known as recharging. Surface water can also dry up if it is overused or if there is a drought. This means that the ground-water can't recharge as quickly as usual.

Sometimes we use groundwater so fast that it doesn't have a chance to recharge. Overusing groundwater for a long period of time isn't good for people or the environment. Overuse can cause the water table to drop. This means that wells must be dug even deeper. It also means that more energy is needed to pump the water to the surface. This makes it more expensive. Using too much groundwater can affect the water levels of streams and river. But there are two even greater dangers of overusing groundwater. They are known as land subsidence and saltwater intrusion.

Groundwater is held in the spaces between gravel, sand, and silt. When the water is removed, the ground can shift down and close the spaces where the water was. The earth settles, or sinks. This is known as land subsidence. It can cause sinkholes to open. It can cause buildings to crack or tilt. One example of this is in San Joaquin Valley, California. In 2015, parts of the valley sank 8 inches (20 centimeters) while other parts sank 13 inches (33 cm) over four to eight months. This resettling of the earth affects the water supply. It lowers the amount of water the ground can absorb and shrinks aquifers.

In cities on the coast, the water table is usually higher than the sea level. But when the water table drops below the sea level, it can cause the ocean water to move inward. This can contaminate fresh-water aquifers. When salt water moves into freshwater, it is called saltwater intrusion. This can contaminate the supply of drinking water.

Some coastal neighborhoods, like this one in New Jersey, have had their drinking water contaminated when salt water gets into the aquifers.

In New Jersey, saltwater intrusion has caused more than 120 water wells to close since the 1940s.

Surface water and groundwater are two separate but connected systems. Groundwater is a popular source of community water. It is usually cheap and easy to collect and use. Groundwater is also less likely to be polluted than surface water. However, polluted groundwater is much harder to clean.

## Water Filtration

All water must be filtered and treated before it is safe to drink. Surface water usually needs more treatment and screening than groundwater. It is more likely to have natural debris in it, like leaves and sticks. Surface water may also have chemicals in it, like the ones that are in some fertilizers. This requires special treatment. Because of these problems, groundwater is a more popular choice for public water. It is usually cleaner so it costs less to make it safe to drink. Today there are many different ways that water can be treated. But most follow the same basic four steps: coagulation and flocculation, sedimentation, filtration, and disinfection.

- **Coagulation and flocculation**: The first step in most water treatment processes is to add chemicals to the water. These chemicals have a positive charge. They join with the negative charge in dirt and other contaminants. They form large clumps called floc.
- **Sedimentation**: The floc is so heavy that it sinks to the bottom of the tanks. This is known as sedimentation.
- **Filtration**: The water is passed through filters made of up of sand, gravel, and charcoal. These filters remove solids, germs, and heavy metals like iron and lead.
- **Disinfection**: Chemicals like chlorine are added to kill any remaining germs and preserve the water pipes.

## Water Fluoridation

Water treatment isn't just about removing harmful materials from water. In the 1950s, health officials decided to try adding something helpful to water. It was a great success. Fluoride is a mineral that appears naturally in some water supplies. It's also one of the main ingredients in toothpaste. Fluoride helps strengthen the outer layer of your teeth. Studies showed that children whose drinking water contained fluoride had about one-third fewer cavities than those who didn't. Health officials started adding small amounts of fluoride to drinking water. They were able to lower rates of tooth decay, especially among poorer people.

# Chapter Three

# WHO OWNS WATER?

In the United States, most people get their water from public water systems. Municipalities usually provide utilities, such as water, to residents. (A municipality is the government of a city or town.) In most cases, they charge a fee based on how much each household is using.

Supplying and maintaining water for a community can cost a lot of money. The federal government does not spend as much money on infrastructure as it used to. At the same time, more and more places need maintenance or even replacement of water systems. Towns must pay for water systems on their own. They can do this by raising the rates on water bills or by raising taxes. These choices are not popular ones.

Often, towns do not have the money to fix their water system. They may decide to allow a private company to take over for a

Many towns use towers like this one to store water. The clean water is pumped into the tower. When it is needed, gravity pulls it back down.

certain amount of time. Sometimes the company buys the water system outright. This is known as water privatization.

## When Towns Go Private

Water privatization can be good for towns because private companies can often afford to upgrade water systems. They can provide safer and more efficient service. Many towns simply cannot afford to entirely replace their old water system. Selling it to a private

Citizens attend a town hall meeting. When towns run the water system, people can have a say about the cost and quality of the system.

company gives the town income along with the upgrades that the system needs. It is important for towns to work with the private companies and make sure they are doing good work. This benefits the town and its residents.

Water privatization can also have its problems. Towns are run by elected officials who serve the public. They do not want to upset the people who vote for them. They will be blamed when costs go up or water quality drops. Private companies, on the other hand, do not have to answer to the public. Private companies are usually focused on making money.

Private companies usually charge much more than public water systems. The city of Bayonne, New Jersey, sold its water system to SUEZ Water. The company promised residents that their water bills would not go up for four years. But after only two years, their rates went up by a lot. Lots of people had a hard time paying their new water bill. SUEZ Water was the only water company in town. They had no reason to keep the rates low.

## Why Towns Choose Not to Privatize Water

For some towns, having a private company run the water system is the right choice. Other times it is not. One of the biggest problems with water privatization is that the people of the town do not have a voice. Also, they often do not know what is happening with the company. As the people of Bayonne found out, companies can make promises they do not keep. Many towns have chosen to privatize and then the company never completes the needed updates.

Private companies and municipalities often have different goals. Municipalities usually want to make sure that every citizen has clean water. Private companies may be more focused on money. In some cases, they may avoid providing service to poor areas. They are worried that the residents will not be able to pay for their service.

## Emmaus for Locally Owned Water

Emmaus is a small town in eastern Pennsylvania. In July 2005, the leaders of Emmaus voted to sell the town's water system. Many people in the town were not happy. They were worried that the water system would be sold to a huge company. They had seen what water privatization had done to other towns in their area. They believed it would not be good for their town. The community started a group called EFLOW: Emmaus for Locally Owned Water. They wrote letters and signed petitions. The group spoke out about their concerns at town meetings. In September, the town voted not to privatize the water system.

Water privatization can be very hard on people who do not have much money. Sometimes people cannot afford to pay their water bill. Private companies may report them to a collection agency. This usually means more fees for the residents. If they cannot pay, people may even lose their homes. Every year, thousands of Americans lose their homes due to unpaid water bills. Municipalities usually do not choose to use collection agencies when a resident cannot pay.

Humans need water to live. People who live in towns with poor water systems cannot choose to simply not use them. In towns with one private water company, residents can't turn somewhere else when they have poor service. Towns with water privatization often lose water

When water prices get too high, people may not be able to pay. They may even lose their homes.

system jobs like repair technicians. This causes the town's unemployment to go up. It also means there are less people to repair and maintain the water system.

## Water Privatization in Atlanta

In 1998, Atlanta, Georgia, signed a contract with United Water. Not long after the company took over the water supply, residents started noticing brown water coming from their taps. They also began receiving advisories to boil their water. This meant that the people of Atlanta had to boil water in order to make it safe for drinking. Each one of these alerts posed a public health risk. The city's water was being contaminated because of issues like water main breaks. In 2003, Atlanta decided to end its contract with United Water after only four years. The city took back control of the water system.

Municipalities learned many lessons from the mistakes that had happened in Atlanta. It is easy to take the water system for granted. But even small problems can have deadly effects. Water privatization can work well. But this can only happen when the companies are well run and think about the citizens that they are serving.

# Chapter Four

# PROTECTING DRINKING WATER

The Cuyahoga River runs through the center of Cleveland, Ohio. On June 22, 1969, it caught fire. The fire caused about $50,000 in damage. The river was polluted with chemicals from nearby factories. It was so bad that there were no fish in the part of the river that runs between Akron and Cleveland. The Cuyahoga was one of the most polluted rivers in America. In Cleveland, the fire wasn't a major new story. The river had caught fire thirteen times before. But this time an article about the fire made its way into *TIME* magazine.

The river fire made the entire country take notice. People realized that more things had to be done to protect the environment. The government passed the Clean Water Act in 1972. It set out

The Cuyahoga River caught fire many times. This photo shows fire-fighters at work on the river in 1952. It caught fire because of the oil and other pollution in the water.

new rules for protecting water from pollution. It also gave the Environmental Protection Agency (EPA) the power to start new programs to control pollution. It was one of the first environmental laws in the country.

In 1974, the Clean Water Act was changed. Scientists who were studying the Mississippi River found thirty-six chemicals in the drinking water. The new law was called the Safe Drinking Water Act. It set standards for "clean" drinking water. This means that any company that provides drinking water must follow certain rules to keep water safe. It also needs to test the water on a regular basis. In 2016, a water crisis in Flint, Michigan, would cause the act to be changed once again.

## Lead Contamination Crisis

In 2014, the city of Flint, Michigan, was looking to save money. The city leaders decided to switch its water supplier. Until then, Flint had gotten its water through the city of Detroit. The water would now come from the Flint River. Shortly after the switch, the people of

Flint noticed their water tasted funny. It also smelled bad. It sometimes had an orange or yellow color to it. City officials told people
to boil their water. The order was stopped after a few weeks, but
residents saw no change in their water.

The Flint water supply system was close to eighty years old. Many
of the pipes that carried water to people's homes were made with
lead. The metal was once often used for plumbing because it was
cheap and easy to work with. In the 1980s, tests showed that lead
is highly toxic to the human body. It was also getting into the water
supply through the lead pipes. Detroit had treated the water with
special chemicals that prevented lead from getting in the water.

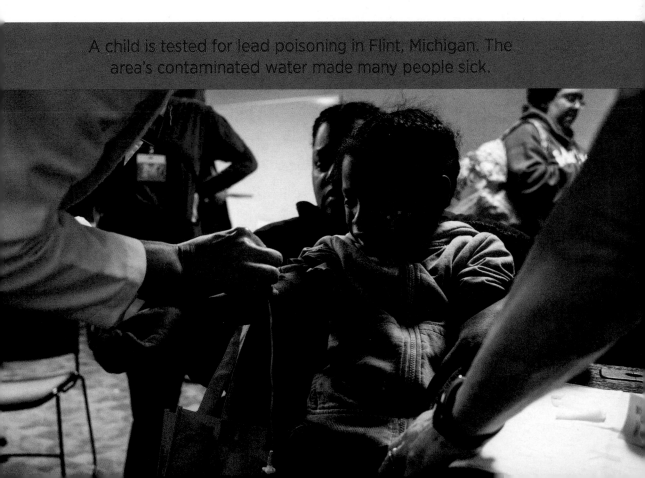

A child is tested for lead poisoning in Flint, Michigan. The
area's contaminated water made many people sick.

But the water from the Flint River was not treated. In 2015, the EPA told state officials that the city's water was contaminated with lead. These warning were ignored for months.

The community of Flint was angry. Many people joined in protests. They demanded change. In January 2016, the mayor declared a state of emergency. A lawsuit was filed. It said that officials had violated the Safe Drinking Water Act. A change was made to the law. It stated that citizens must be told right away when water is found to be contaminated with lead.

## Lead Poisoning

Lead is a heavy metal. When it enters the human body, it can cause stomach illness, brain damage, hearing loss, and even death. In the 1970s, a doctor studied young children who were exposed to lead. He found that it led to learning disabilities, aggression, and lowered IQ. During the Flint water crisis, between six thousand and twelve thousand children were exposed to lead. Some children had such high levels of lead in their blood that they had rashes. Some of the effects of lead poisoning can be reversed. Many cannot.

## Environmental Justice

The Clean Water Act changed the way people thought about the environment. It was one of the first times the government had responded to citizens who were worried about the environment. Many people saw the act as justice for the environment. They said that it protected communities from pollution. Before the act, poor and

Native Americans protest the building of the Dakota Pipeline in 2016.

minority communities were much more likely to be exposed to pollution and contaminated water. The act did improve the quality of water around the country. But there are still areas that need to be improved.

## Environmental Injustice

In 2014, an oil and gas company announced plans to build a new pipeline. The company was Energy Transfer Partners (ETP). The underground pipeline would move almost half a million barrels of oil between North Dakota and Illinois. The original route for the pipeline passed close to the water supply of Bismarck, North Dakota.

This meant an oil leak or spill could hurt the city's water supply. ETP chose to change the route of the pipeline. The new route crossed under the Missouri River. It ran only 500 feet (152 meters) from the Standing Rock Indian Reservation. The route change meant the pipeline could harm the reservation's water supply. The Standing Rock Sioux tribe spoke out against the pipeline. The EPA asked for a new study to be done before the pipeline was built.

ETP refused to do a new study. It began building the pipeline. The tribe turned to the courts to stop construction. Still, ETP continued to build as the court cases went on. In August 2016, peaceful protesters gathered to block the construction.

Soon the entire country knew about the protests. Security guards hired by ETP were filmed using pepper spray and attack dogs on the protestors. In cities across the country, people showed support for the protestors who would not back down. In November, local police were shown using water hoses and rubber bullets on the protestors. Nearly three hundred people were hurt over the course of the protest. Just before his term ended, President Obama ordered pipeline construction to stop until an environmental study was done.

Shortly after Donald Trump became president, he signed an order allowing construction under the river to begin. The pipeline was completed in April 2017. By the time it was done, it had already had two oil leaks. Many worry that the pipeline will hurt the water supply of the Native American people.

# Chapter Five

# CLIMATE CHANGE AND THE WATER SUPPLY

Water is a natural resource. This means that anything that affects nature will also affect the water supply. Scientists are just starting to understand how climate change is affecting our planet. Rising temperatures greatly affect the water cycle. This means different things for different areas. The West Coast often has droughts and less rain. The East Coast has heavy rains that lead to flooding. In all parts of the world, climate change is a very real threat to the water supply.

## Water Supply and Demand

When temperatures go up, water evaporates faster. On a hot day, your body needs more water than normal to keep your body temperature from rising. Food crops also need more water when it

Taxis in a parking lot in Hoboken, New Jersey. Major flooding happened as a result of Superstorm Sandy in 2012.

is hot. At the same time, the atmosphere is holding more water because of greenhouse gases. This means it takes longer for water in the air to return to the earth as rain or snow. As the population rises, the demand for safe drinking water will rise with it. At the same time the demand for water is rising, many areas will have less water.

Droughts and less rain can cause communities to overuse groundwater. As you read in chapter two, overuse of groundwater can cause aquifers to collapse. This lowers the amount of freshwater that can be stored within the earth. Rising oceans can harm coastal freshwater aquifers. When rivers begin to dry up, salt water moves further inland. This raises the salt level of the freshwater in that area.

Many places depend on moving water in rivers to create hydroelectricity. When droughts cause the rivers to lower, towns might not be able to make enough electricity. This can lead to power outages. A lack of snow can have the same effect as a lack of rain. Some rivers are fed throughout the summer by melting mountain glaciers. But what happens if the mountains don't get enough snowfall? Or the snow melts too early in the season? There will be less water in the summer when temperatures are usually at their peak.

## Water Quality

As temperatures rise, severe weather events like hurricanes and floods become more common. Water treatment systems can only handle so much water at once. Heavy rain can overload these systems. This can allow untreated water and sewage to get into the supply of drinking water. Heavy rain also increases the amount of runoff

A hydroelectric dam uses water to create power for areas nearby.

entering rivers. The runoff pollutes the rivers. After periods of heavy rain, high amounts of chemicals used in farming are swept into rivers.

Fertilizer is not usually harmful. But too much fertilizer can be a disaster for water quality. Fertilizer adds nutrients to water that can cause algae blooms. These can create a toxic chemical that can hurt sea life as well as humans. Breaking waves can cause the toxins to enter the air. They can irritate the eyes, nose, and throat. Algae blooms leave behind a bacteria that lowers the amount of oxygen in the water. Fish and other sea life depend on the oxygen in water the same way humans depend on air.

Two photos show the same area in Oroville, California, three years apart. The bottom picture shows the effects of severe drought.

## Drought in California

Droughts happen a lot in California. But the time between December 2011 and March 2017 was the driest in the state's history. Supplies of water for agriculture were cut by 50 percent as aquifers began to collapse. Two-thirds of all American fruit and nuts are grown in California. As the drought went on, the state tried many different ways to save water. Heavy rains at the start of 2017 were both good and bad. They caused flooding in many cities but they also helped end the drought. Many climate scientists fear climate change will cause more droughts like this.

# An Unending Cycle

One of the reasons scientists think climate change is speeding up is because it feeds on itself. Rising temperatures make ocean water evaporate faster. This makes the oceans' temperatures rise faster. As water becomes hard to get in some parts of the country, it must be shipped from other areas. The fuel used to ship water adds gases to the atmosphere. This helps temperatures rise. Scientists all over the world are working on ways to slow down the effects of climate change before it's too late. New businesses are focusing on renewable energy and conservation. They are working on ways to solve the problems of today and tomorrow.

## California Wildfires

In 2017, California's worst drought ever finally ended. The same year, the state also had one of the worst wildfire seasons on record. California has a dry climate and lots of forests. This means that wildfires can happen often. But in 2017, more than nine thousand fires burned over a million acres (404,685 hectares) of the state. Five of the state's twenty worst fires happened in 2017. In 2014, scientists said that climate change was a reason for the rising number of fires in California.

# Chapter Six

# THE FUTURE OF WATER

When it comes to climate change, the future of water seems bleak. Scientists say that as the temperature goes up, our water supply will continue to go down. But there is hope to be found as well. Many people are working on ways to make sure our water will not run out. This means finding ways to save the water we have. It also means discovering new ways of accessing water.

Water is becoming big business. In recent years, droughts have begun to hurt the water supply. All around the world, people need to do a better job of managing and conserving water. This has led to many new jobs in these areas. This chapter will introduce you to the future of jobs in the water supply industry.

In 2017, large crowds gathered in Washington, DC, to demand that the government do more about climate change.

## Labor Shortages

The water industry is facing some big problems. One of these is the idea that jobs in water and waste management are not valued. But these jobs are so important for the health and safety of communities. The idea that these are not "good jobs" has led to a lack of interest. Many companies have a hard time filling job openings. But people are slowly starting to see the value in this work. Companies are beginning to attract more workers to the field.

# Plumbers

As America tries to fix its old water infrastructure, the need for skilled people like plumbers will rise. Plumbers build and maintain any system that carries fluids. They are a key part of public health and safety. Plumbers make sure that water systems are protected from pipe problems like lead poisoning. By maintaining the water systems, they also help conserve water by preventing leaks. In the future, plumbers will be needed to remove the lead pipes that are still remaining in America's water infrastructure.

# Solving the Water Shortage Problem

Droughts are becoming more common around the globe. We need more people working to solve the problem. We need experts like environmental scientists and water engineers. They can help figure out the best ways to conserve and use the water supply. Water conservation jobs like rainwater harvesting, recycling wastewater, and urban runoff will also become more important. These scientists work together to find the best ways to get water to areas in need.

# Water Quality Technicians

Climate change causes severe storms and rising sea levels. These things threaten the water quality all over the world. Water quality technicians do chemical tests to check the levels of contamination

A group of engineers goes over plans at a water treatment center.

in drinking water. They make sure that water supplies meet today's standards for clean water. They also find new ways to control and protect against pollutants.

# Hydrologists

Hydrologists are scientists who study the qualities of water. They try to solve all the water problems facing the planet today. These scientists do work in the lab using computers. They also spend a good deal of time in the field gathering information about the water system. Hydrologists look to solve erosion problems caused by drought and flooding. They help public health officials and environmental scientists check the quality of local water supplies. The more we understand about our planet's water system, the better we can manage it.

## Shade Balls

In 2008, water quality technicians needed a way to slow evaporation in a California reservoir. They were trying to prevent the spread of toxic algae blooms. They came up with a creative solution. They poured four hundred thousand black plastic balls, known as shade balls, on top of the reservoir. The balls blocked the sun's rays from reaching the water. This slowed the evaporation and stopped the spread of the algae. They had gotten the idea from airports that had been using a similar method to keep birds from landing in ponds around airports.

# Weather Forecasting

The weather is something humans depend on. It is also something

Water is an essential resource. All people must do
their part to make sure that we do not waste it.

we have no control over. In the past, communities had to make
water management plans based on the hope that rain would
come. Atmospheric scientists study and predict the weather and
climate. Advances in weather forecasting and satellite pictures
now help weather forecasters predict the weather sooner. In the
past, forecasters could predict the weather one day away. Now
they can predict the weather five days ahead. Severe storms are
becoming stronger and more common. This means we need more

people who are experts on the weather. Early forecasting gives towns more time to prepare or evacuate in the case of severe weather events. In times of drought, early and accurate predictions help towns plan better. They also allow farmers to protect crops from frost and droughts.

## The Future of Our Water Supply

Our water supply is one of the nation's most valuable resources. When we have plenty of it, we do not give it much thought. But events like the California droughts and the Flint water crisis have reminded us how important it is to protect our water supply. Conservation efforts and infrastructure improvements can help protect our water supply for years to come. It is up to future generations to continue to find new and better ways to use and manage this valuable resource.

# CHRONOLOGY

**1804**  Sand water filters are developed in Scotland.

**1854**  Dr. John Snow proves cholera is spread through contaminated drinking water.

**1908**  America begins to use chlorine to disinfect water.

**1945**  First town in America begins adding fluoride to drinking water.

**1972**  Congress passes the Clean Water Act.

**1974**  Congress passes the Safe Drinking Water Act.

**1988**  Congress passes the Lead Contamination Control Act.

**2016**  Congress passes the Water Infrastructure Improvements for the Nation Act.

# GLOSSARY

**aquifer**  A body of rock that can contain or transmit groundwater.

**contaminate**  To make something impure by adding poisonous elements.

**erosion**  The gradual wearing away of soil or stones.

**freshwater**  Water that doesn't contain salt.

**groundwater**  Water held underground in the soil or in pores and crevices in rock.

**hydrologist**  A scientist who studies the movement and distribution of water.

**infrastructure**  The basic things needed for the operation of a society.

**pandemic**  A disease that has spread all over the world.

**privy**  A toilet located in a small shed outside a house or other building; an outhouse.

**saltwater intrusion**  When salt water pushes inland and contaminates groundwater supplies.

**subsidence**  The gradual caving in or sinking of an area of land.

**surface water**  Water that collects on the surface of the ground.

**water cycle**  The cycle of processes by which water circulates between the earth's oceans, atmosphere, and land.

**water table**  The level below which the ground is saturated with water.

# FURTHER READING

## Books

Berne, Emma Carlson. *From River to Raindrop: The Water Cycle.* Minneapolis, MN: Lerner, 2017.

Herman, Gail. *What Is Climate Change?* New York, NY: Penguin, 2018.

Stewart, Melissa. *Water.* Washington, DC: National Geographic, 2014.

Yomtov, Nel. *Water/Wastewater Engineer.* Ann Arbor, MI: Cherry Lake, 2015.

## Websites

**charity: water**

*www.charitywater.org*

The nonprofit organization charity: water attempts to bring clean water to developing nations.

**Clean Water Action**

*www.cleanwateraction.org*

This nonprofit is dedicated to protecting the nation's water supply.

**Environmental Protection Agency**

*www.epa.gov*

The EPA's mission is to protect human health and the environment.

# INDEX